Friends
for a Lifetime

Love

Joy

Happiness

Caring

Sharing

Kindness

Understanding

Memories

© 2001 Havoc Publishing
San Diego, California
U.S.A.

ISBN 0-7416-1922-9
Text by Kathy Cisneros

www.havocpub.com

Made in Korea

This book is dedicated to
the everlasting friendship of

_____

and

_____

Meeting you changed

my life in so many ways.

How It All Began

From the moment we met there was a connection. The story of our friendship began when: _____

_____

_____

I will never forget the place we first met: _____

_____

Meeting you changed my life in so many ways: _____

_____

_____

We shared so many of the same thoughts! It was as if you could read my mind. I remember once: _____

_____

_____

Do you remember the way we always finished each other's sentences? It was so funny the way I would say:

_____

_____

Sometimes looking at you was like looking into a mirror. I saw myself in you because: _____

_____

_____

_____

History

When we talked about our parents and our nationalities, you taught me that: _____

_____

_____

_____

_____

_____

One of us had to be the leader while the other would follow. Most of the time the leader was: _____

_____

_____

You saw past the physical and liked me for who I was inside. For the first time in my life, I felt: _____

_____

_____

_____

You had a way with words that put me at ease. I knew I could always find my lost smile in your eyes. You

always made me laugh when you: _____

_____

_____

I remember how sensitive you were to: _____

_____

_____

_____

You had

a way

with words

that put me at ease.

We spent so much time together

laughing and supporting each other.

Making Time For Friendship

You welcomed me and my long conversations even when you: _____

_____

_____

At times I thought I would wear out my welcome in your heart, but you always set my worries at ease by:

_____

_____

_____

I felt as though I had found a kindred spirit because of the way you: _____

_____

_____

I remember telling you things I could never tell my own mother! Do you remember when we talked about:

_____

_____

_____

You even told me things that were sacred to your heart. I remember once you shared: _____

_____

_____

We spent so much time together laughing and supporting each other. Do you remember how people

would say: _____

_____

Place photograph here

Place photograph here

You Know

I don't even have to say it,

You know just how I feel.

You understand the things in me,

sometimes I don't reveal.

You support me with encouragement

and will not let me fall.

You help me face the world each day.

You help me face it all.

How did you ever find me?

You make it all seem right.

We hardly ever argue,

We rarely ever fight.

You make me see things I forgot,

and then I know it's true.

I'm so grateful that you found me,

and so glad,

that I found you!

Favorites

You wanted me to try new things that you liked. I remember once you tried to make me eat: _____

_____

I made a recipe you kept begging me for but I would never give up my secret! Here's the one you always

wanted: _____

_____

_____

_____

_____

_____

Just the other day I saw our favorite movie on TV. It reminded me so much of us and really captured the

essence of our relationship. Even the title:_____

means so much to me because:_____

_____

Remember that actor you talked about constantly? It used to drive me crazy when you wouldn't stop talking

about: _____

_____

Even our soap operas were in sync. Your favorite was: _____ But I liked: _____

because:_____

Even our soap operas

were in sync.

You have

such a unique

sense of fashion!

Fashion Bugs

You have such a unique sense of fashion! One time you got the nerve to wear: _____

out in public! Whenever I walked down the street with you I felt:_____

_____

_____

_____

_____

_____

_____

_____

You loved those shoes that hurt my feet so much to wear. I wore them constantly because they made me feel

like: _____

_____

_____

_____

_____

Fragrances

Your signature perfume was: _____

_____

My choice of perfume captured me as well. My favorite will always be: _____

_____

_____

_____

Every time I pass a florist, I can't help thinking about your favorite flower. You even remind me of a:

_____

because: _____

_____

_____

My special flower will always be a:_____ It brings back memories of: _____

_____

_____

_____

_____

Remember when I gave you a bouquet of: _____ to celebrate: _____

_____

_____

_____

Fashion Bugs

You have such a unique sense of fashion! One time you got the nerve to wear: _____

out in public! Whenever I walked down the street with you I felt:_____

_____

_____

_____

_____

_____

_____

_____

You loved those shoes that hurt my feet so much to wear. I wore them constantly because they made me feel

like: _____

_____

_____

_____

Place photograph here

Place photograph here

Fragrances

Your signature perfume was: _____

_____

My choice of perfume captured me as well. My favorite will always be: _____

_____

_____

_____

Every time I pass a florist, I can't help thinking about your favorite flower. You even remind me of a:

_____

because: _____

_____

_____

My special flower will always be a:_____ It brings back memories of: _____

_____

_____

_____

Remember when I gave you a bouquet of: _____ to celebrate: _____

_____

_____

_____

The perfume

that you gave me as

a gift,

soon became

my favorite.

Somehow I knew

I'd never grow

old in your eyes.

Celebrations

Somehow I knew I'd never grow old in your eyes. You always see me as a: _____

_____

_____

_____

_____

Remember when we celebrated your birthday by: _____

_____

_____

You always counted the days until: _____ because: _____

_____

_____

With your special touch, you made each holiday more meaningful because: _____

_____

_____

_____

Remember when on a gift exchange, I gave you a: _____

 and you gave me a: _____

_____

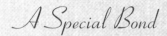

A Special Bond

Your face was so familiar,
as though I always knew.
We were just so meant to be,
a bond between us two.

We're always just a reach away,
through an e-mail or a call.
We never let each other fail,
Together, we stand tall.

We'll always be united,
we're stuck as if by glue.
And I am proud,
cause I'm allowed,
to walk the world with you!

We were
just so

meant to be.

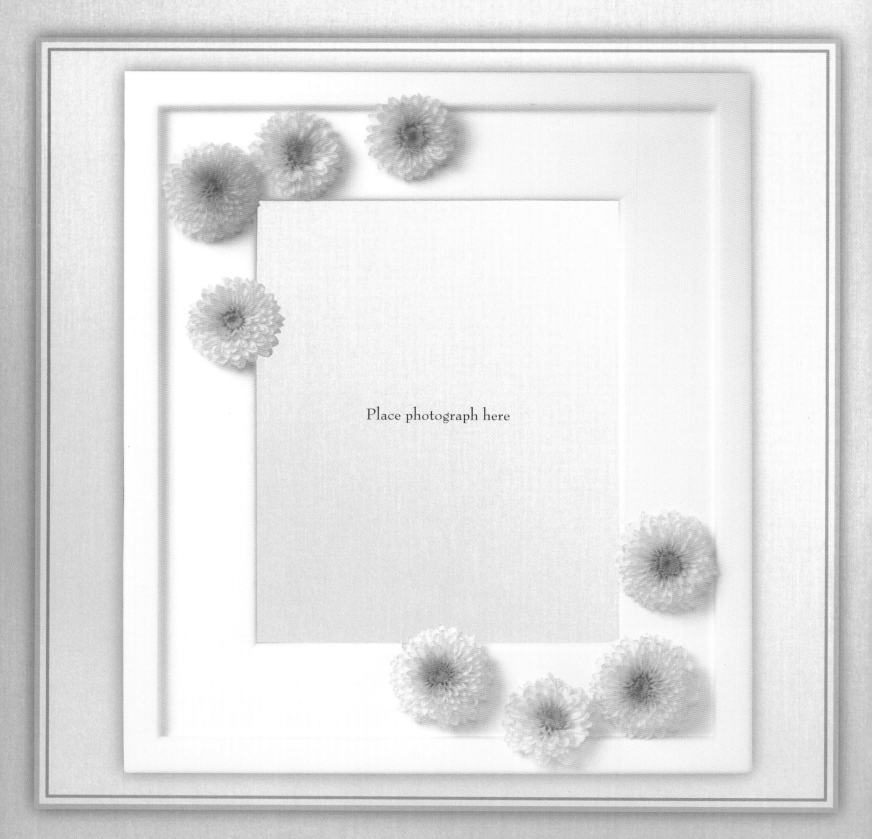

Place photograph here

Place photograph here

Each card you sent

me meant so much.

Way With Words

Each card you sent me meant so much because: _____

_____

_____

_____

I saved all the letters you ever wrote me because: _____

_____

_____

When I'm feeling a little blue, I look back through my scrapbooks and journals and find your words of

wisdom to me. You always lift my spirit because of the way you: _____

_____

_____

Both of us faced trying times in our lives. I remember feeling devastated when I found out that you: _____

_____

I remember not knowing what to say or how to approach the sadness in your heart. You set me at ease the

moment you said:_____

_____

Sometimes just knowing you'll be there for me no matter what is enough to give me courage. One time

when I faced: _____

_____

_____

Music

Remember when we first met, this song was so popular: _____

We both loved to dance so much! How could we ever forget: _____

_____

_____

_____

_____

Whenever we heard the song: _____ ,neither one of us could help: _____

_____

My favorite group to dance to will always be:_____

While I know you can't help moving to: _____

_____

Our favorite place to sit back and listen to music will always be: _____

_____

_____

If I had to pick one song that reminded me of our friendship it would be: _____

because: _____

_____

_____

_____

Your friendship

is a treasure.

Your Touch

You always know what to say to me,

whenever my skies turn to gray.

I always know you'll comfort me,

with those precious words you say.

You touch me with your tenderness,

and you forever understand.

You always give hope back to me,

as though you had it planned.

$\mathcal{Y}$our friendship is a treasure,

there's love in all you touch.

Each moment I have spent with you

just means, so very much.

So if sometimes I don't show it,

please know you'll always be,

a precious part of every day,

that means the world to me.

You have such

an infectious giggle.

Laughter

People can't help but laugh along with you when you're in one of your spells! Remember the time: _____

_____

_____

_____

I was so embarrassed when you laughed at: _____

_____

_____

_____

When we were both laughing, we'd turn bright shades of red and the more we tried to stop, the harder it was.

I remember when we burst out laughing because of: _____

_____

_____

Even though we didn't want people gossiping about us, we couldn't help talking about: _____

_____

_____

Can you believe all the things I told you about: _____

_____

_____

Our favorite gossip topic of all time will always be: _____

_____

Place photograph here

Place photograph here

Games

Why were we always so competitive when we played: _____

_____

_____

_____

I think your secret to always winning was: _____

_____

_____

_____

_____

I think we both knew the reason I wanted to keep score all the time was: _____

_____

_____

_____

_____

I remember a time when we were on the same team up against: _____

_____

Our favorite game to play together is: _____ because: _____

_____

_____

With you on my
team, we can

never lose.

Without You

Where would I be without you?

Who else would put up with me?

You are the only one who knows,

my unique personality!

You comprehend the little things,

that no one ever gets.

You let me make mistakes, but

never let me have regrets.

You take me where, I wouldn't dare be

when I'm alone.

And if I'm ever blue for you,

I just pick up the phone!

So don't you ever take away,

this magic that you do.

For I'm blessed in every way,

with the friend,

I've found in you.

We always had nicknames

for each other.

Nicknames

I almost died laughing the first time you called me: _____

_____

_____

I guess I earned that nickname because: _____

_____

_____

_____

_____

You were surprised when I christened you with the nickname of: _____

_____

_____

_____

_____

You earned your nickname by: _____

_____

_____

_____

_____

_____

Place photograph here

Differences

The only one of us who will ever be organized is: _____

because of the time: _____

_____

_____

_____

The tone deaf singer between us simply has to be: _____

because of the time: _____

_____

_____

The best actress award has to go to: _____ because of the time: _____

_____

_____

_____

The most different thing from you to me is: _____

_____

_____

Why I like your differences and how I've learned from them: _____

_____

_____

_____

_____

You

I can cry when I'm with you.
Your shoulder is there for me.
I don't have to hide
My feelings inside,
You give me security.

When I can't endure,
the world much more
You tell me to behave.
You hold me up
When I am weak,
And I'm about to cave.

𝒴ou don't hold back,
You speak the truth,
And tell me when I'm wrong.
You make me feel,
Part of your life,
As though I do belong.

I cherish all your wisdom,
And times that we have shared.
You never let me once forget,
How much you really cared.

I hope I give the same to you,
And that you'll always be,
In my life as you are now,
Together, you and me.

Quiet Times

Sometimes whether it's silent conversations over coffee or paused moments during phone conversations, we can read each other's hearts so well. I remember once when:_____

_____

_____

_____

_____

I can always tell when you're sad by the way you: _____

_____

_____

You can always see my unhappiness because of the way you know: _____

_____

_____

I was so happy for you when you received the news about: _____

_____

_____

_____

We always celebrated special moments in our lives by: _____

_____

_____

_____

We can read each other's

hearts so well.

Place photograph here

Place photograph here

I didn't want

you to give

up your dream.

Careers

You were always meant to be a: _____

because of the way you: _____

_____

I grew into my position at: _____ and learned to realize that: _____

_____

_____

I didn't want you to give up on your dream of becoming a: _____

_____

_____

You wouldn't allow me to give up on my dream of becoming a: _____

_____

_____

If I had to do it all over again in another lifetime, the things I would do differently are: _____

_____

You told me once you always thought you'd turn out to be: _____

_____

I picture you more as a: _____ because of the way you: _____

_____

You always saw me as: _____ because you said: _____

_____

This Way

Oh, how you make me laugh sometimes!
Oh, how you make me sad!
No one else in the world but you,
can get me quite so mad!

I guess it's because of how close we are,
you know me oh so well.
Whenever you are sad inside,
my heart can always tell.

It's a silent bond that goes beyond,
the things we do and say.
I hope we'll always have this love
and it will always be this way!

I look forward to tomorrow because I have a friend like you in my life.

Habits

You have one habit that drives me crazy because: _____

_____

_____

_____

Why does it bother you so much when I: _____

_____

_____

_____

For our own good, we both need to stop: _____

I think it would benefit us both because: _____

_____

_____

_____

We always come up with the most creative ways to save money. Remember when you: _____

_____

_____

You laughed so hard when you found out I: _____

_____

We both saved a few bucks by: _____

_____

_____

You Renew

One moment in your company,
can bring out my largest smile.
You have a way, to make me play
and giggle for awhile.

My stress is gone, when I am drawn
to what you have to say.
You reach into the pain I knew
and throw it all away.

You inspire each day brand new,
each time you smile and show,
the friendship that you have for me,
The love we've come to know.

You can bring out
                    my largest smile.

Feelings

When someone hurts you, they hurt me, too. It broke my heart when:_____

_____

_____

_____

_____

I know you will always defend me because of the time: _____

_____

_____

_____

We always stand up for each other like the time when: _____

_____

_____

_____

We always forgive and forget our flaws because deep down, we really love each other. Remember the time

after we had a big fight, we made up by promising: _____

_____

_____

_____

_____

When someone hurts
you, they hurt
me, too.

I promise to always be there

when you need me.

Promises

I promise to always be there when you need me. Just like the time when: _____

_____

_____

_____

I know you will always be there for me as well.   Like the time when you: _____

_____

_____

_____

When you have a special moment to share with the world, don't forget to call me. I want to share in your

happiness because: _____

_____

When I feel lonely and all alone against the world, I'll remember your name and what we have meant to

each other. Your friendship to me has meant: _____

_____

 I look forward to tomorrow because I have a friend like you in my life. I will always be grateful for you

because you have given me: _____

_____

_____

_____

Friendship for a Lifetime

A friendship for a lifetime,

with love between us two,

is what I have in knowing,

a special friend like you!